A New Baby Brother

by Libby McCord

illustrated by Doreen Gay Kassel

Scott Foresman
is an imprint of

PEARSON

Glenview, Illinois • Boston, Massachusetts • Chandler, Arizona
Upper Saddle River, New Jersey

Illustrations by Doreen Gay Kassel

ISBN 13: 978-0-328-50780-1
ISBN 10:   0-328-50780-6

9 10 V010 15 14 13

I am Marco. This is my dad.
See the picture? That is my family.
Soon, we will have a new baby.

This is my mom. She spends lots of time with me.

"Will she still have time with the new baby?" I thought.

"Mom, will you still take me to the park?" I asked.

"I will take you and the baby to the park," Mom said.

This is my bedroom. "Where will the baby sleep?" I asked.

"In your room with you," said Dad. "I remember when I stood at the door to watch you sleep."

This is my baby brother. He is cute.
I share my dad's lap with my brother.
I am a good big brother.

A Care Book

Read Together

Make a picture album of people you love and care about. It can hold photographs of you and your family. Or, it can be a book of your drawings of people you love. You can call it your Care Book.

Think about the people you love most. Find pictures or make some of yourself doing things you like with your family or friends. Write the names of everybody in your pictures. Make up sentences about what you are doing in the pictures.

Take your Care Book home. Show it to all the people you love.